PAUL GILBERT

The Chaplet of the Divine Mercy

Includes Message, Devotions and Powerful Divine Mercy Prayers for Healing, Miracles and More

Copyright © 2023 by Paul Gilbert

All rights reserved. No part of this publication may be reproduced, stored or transmitted in any form or by any means, electronic, mechanical, photocopying, recording, scanning, or otherwise without written permission from the publisher. It is illegal to copy this book, post it to a website, or distribute it by any other means without permission.

First edition

*This book was professionally typeset on Reedsy.
Find out more at reedsy.com*

Contents

1	Introduction	1
2	Understanding the Divine Mercy Devotion	6
3	The Chaplet's Structure and Components	14
4	How to Begin Praying the Chaplet	21
5	Praying the Chaplet: A Closer Look	25
6	Special Intentions and Novena	29
7	The Promises and Graces of the Chaplet	35
8	Praying the Chaplet as a Community	40
9	Troubleshooting and Common Questions	43
10	Living the Divine Mercy Message	50
11	Conclusion	57

1

Introduction

The Divine Mercy Chaplet is a profound and cherished prayer in the Catholic faith, with its origin and significance deeply rooted in the spiritual journey of a humble Polish nun, Saint Faustina Kowalska, and the divine messages she received. Here is a compelling explanation of its origin and significance:

Origin:

The story of the Divine Mercy Chaplet begins in the early 20th century when Sister Faustina, born Helena Kowalska, entered the Congregation of the Sisters of Our Lady of Mercy in Warsaw, Poland. In the solitude of her convent life, she had mystical experiences and received profound revelations from Jesus Christ. These revelations urged her to spread a message of God's mercy to the world.

Significance:

1. Message of Mercy: At the heart of the Divine Mercy Chaplet is the message of God's unfathomable mercy for all humanity. Sister Faustina's visions of Jesus emphasized the depth of His

love and forgiveness, encouraging us to trust in His mercy and turn to Him in times of need.

2. Prayers for Repentance: The Chaplet consists of prayers that invoke God's mercy upon sinners. It is a powerful tool for seeking forgiveness and reconciliation with God, reminding us that no sin is too great for His boundless mercy.

3. Healing and Comfort: The Chaplet provides comfort to those suffering physically, emotionally, or spiritually. It serves as a source of hope and consolation, reminding us that God is always ready to embrace us in our times of pain and sorrow.

4. Universal Prayer: The Divine Mercy Chaplet is a universal prayer, not restricted to a particular time or place. It can be recited by individuals or in community, fostering a sense of unity among believers worldwide in their plea for mercy.

5. Feast of Divine Mercy: Pope John Paul II, recognizing the importance of this devotion, established the Feast of Divine Mercy, celebrated on the Sunday after Easter. This feast further highlights the significance of the Chaplet, emphasizing the resurrection and the mercy of Christ.

6. Promises and Blessings: Sister Faustina received promises from Jesus for those who recite the Chaplet with faith. These promises include the assurance of God's mercy and the grace of a peaceful death.

In summary, the Divine Mercy Chaplet is not merely a prayer; it is a profound revelation of God's love and mercy for humanity.

INTRODUCTION

It invites believers to trust in the boundless compassion of God, seek His forgiveness, and become instruments of His mercy in a world often burdened by sin and suffering. The Chaplet's origin in the spiritual experiences of Sister Faustina and its profound significance in the Catholic faith make it a powerful and transformative aspect of Christian devotion.

Readers of "A Guide to Praying the Chaplet of the Divine Mercy" can anticipate a transformative journey into the heart of one of the most profound and cherished devotions in the Catholic faith. This book offers a compelling overview of what readers can expect to learn and achieve:

1. Deep Understanding of the Divine Mercy Devotion:
   - Gain a comprehensive understanding of the history, theology, and significance of the Divine Mercy devotion, tracing its origins from the life of St. Faustina Kowalska to its place in modern Catholic spirituality.

2. Step-by-Step Guidance on Praying the Chaplet:
   - Receive clear, step-by-step instructions on how to pray the Divine Mercy Chaplet, making it accessible to both newcomers and those seeking a deeper connection with this prayer.

3. Spiritual Growth and Personal Transformation:
   - Learn how to infuse your prayer life with profound spirituality and experience personal transformation by embracing the message of God's mercy, forgiveness, and love.

4. Overcoming Common Challenges:

- Discover practical tips for overcoming common challenges and distractions during prayer, enabling you to maintain focus and deepen your connection with God.

5. Integration into Daily Life:
 - Explore ways to integrate the Divine Mercy Chaplet and its principles into your daily life, helping you embody mercy, compassion, and forgiveness in your interactions with others.

6. Powerful Testimonials and Real-Life Stories:
 - Be inspired by real-life stories and testimonials of individuals who have experienced the transformative power of the Divine Mercy Chaplet, deepening your faith and trust in God's mercy.

7. The Promises and Graces:
 - Gain insights into the promises and blessings associated with the Chaplet, offering you hope and assurance in God's unwavering love and mercy.

8. Community and Group Praying:
 - Learn how to organize or participate in Divine Mercy prayer groups, fostering a sense of community and shared devotion with others.

9. Resource for Ongoing Spiritual Growth:
 - Use this book as a valuable resource for continued spiritual growth, with sample prayers, glossaries, and references to deepen your knowledge of the Divine Mercy devotion.

In essence, this book serves as a guiding light for individuals seeking to explore, understand, and embrace the Divine Mercy

INTRODUCTION

Chaplet, both as a powerful prayer and as a transformative way of life. Through its pages, readers will find not only the means to enrich their spiritual journey but also a path towards a more profound experience of God's boundless love and mercy.

2

Understanding the Divine Mercy Devotion

Title: A History of Divine Mercy: The Life of St. Faustina Kowalska and the Devotion

Introduction

The Divine Mercy devotion stands as a beacon of hope and compassion in the Catholic faith, offering solace and strength through the depths of God's unfathomable mercy. Central to this devotion is the remarkable life of Saint Faustina Kowalska, whose experiences and messages from Christ shaped the foundation of this spiritual movement. In this exploration, we journey through the history and background of the Divine Mercy devotion, shining a light on the life and mission of St. Faustina Kowalska.

The Early Life of Helena Kowalska

Helena Kowalska, later known as Saint Faustina, was born on

August 25, 1905, in Głogowiec, a small village in Poland. Raised in a devout Catholic family, she was the third of ten children. From a young age, Helena exhibited a strong inclination towards piety and prayer, her heart deeply drawn to the divine.

Answering the Call to Religious Life

At the age of 19, Helena felt a profound calling to dedicate her life to God. She left her family and home, setting forth on a spiritual journey that eventually led her to the Congregation of the Sisters of Our Lady of Mercy in Warsaw in 1925. She was given the religious name Sister Maria Faustina of the Most Blessed Sacrament, signifying her lifelong commitment to serving Christ.

Mystical Experiences and Visions

Sister Faustina's spiritual journey was marked by profound mystical experiences and visions, often involving conversations with Jesus Christ. Beginning in 1931, she received a series of extraordinary revelations that would later form the cornerstone of the Divine Mercy devotion. In one of her most famous visions, Jesus appeared to her as the "King of Divine Mercy," with rays of red and pale light radiating from His heart.

The Divine Mercy Image

Perhaps the most iconic element of the Divine Mercy devotion is the image of Jesus as He appeared to Sister Faustina in her visions. Jesus instructed her to have a painting made of this image, which depicts Him with His right hand raised in blessing and His left hand touching His heart, from which two rays – one red and one pale – emanate. The red ray symbolizes the Blood of Jesus, and the pale ray represents the Water of Baptism, both signifying the mercy and love of God for all humanity. Beneath the image are the words "Jesus, I trust in You," a central message of the devotion.

The Divine Mercy Chaplet

One of the key elements of the Divine Mercy devotion is the Divine Mercy Chaplet. In her visions, Sister Faustina received instructions from Jesus on how to pray this powerful and deeply transformative prayer. The Chaplet consists of a series of prayers and meditations that invoke God's mercy upon sinners and the whole world. It is a simple yet profound prayer that encourages trust in God's mercy, seeks forgiveness, and imparts a sense of hope and consolation to those who pray it.

The Mission of Divine Mercy

Through her mystical experiences, Sister Faustina understood her mission was to spread the message of God's mercy to the world. She recorded her experiences, conversations with Christ, and prayers in a diary, known as the "Diary of Saint Maria Faustina Kowalska." This diary became a vital source of inspiration for the Divine Mercy devotion, offering spiritual insights and guidance to countless individuals.

Facing Challenges and Misunderstanding

Sister Faustina's mission was not without its challenges. She faced skepticism and misunderstanding from some within the Church, who questioned the authenticity of her experiences and the devotion. However, she persevered, placing her trust in God's plan and continuing to spread the message of divine mercy.

The Spread of the Divine Mercy Devotion

Despite the challenges, the message of Divine Mercy began to spread. In 1935, the first Divine Mercy image was publicly displayed in Vilnius, Lithuania. In the years that followed, devotion to the Divine Mercy Chaplet and the image gained momentum. The devotion was further popularized by the writings of St. Faustina and the efforts of her spiritual directors, particularly Father Michael Sopoćko.

Recognition by the Church

In the years following St. Faustina's death in 1938, the Divine Mercy devotion began to receive recognition and approval from the Catholic Church. In the 1950s, a canonical investigation was initiated into her life and writings, which ultimately led to her beatification in 1993 and her canonization as a saint by Pope John Paul II in the year 2000. This recognition by the Church served as a significant endorsement of the authenticity of the Divine Mercy devotion.

The Feast of Divine Mercy

To further emphasize the importance of the Divine Mercy devotion, Pope John Paul II declared the Second Sunday of Easter as the Feast of Divine Mercy, now celebrated throughout the Catholic Church. This feast underscores the significance of Christ's resurrection and the message of God's mercy, culminating in the Sunday of Mercy.

Impact and Significance of the Divine Mercy Devotion

The Divine Mercy devotion continues to have a profound impact on the lives of believers worldwide. It serves as a reminder of the infinite love and mercy of God, a beacon of hope in a world often burdened by sin and suffering. The Chaplet, the image, and the message of Divine Mercy offer solace and strength, encouraging individuals to seek forgiveness, trust in God, and become instruments of His mercy in the world.

Conclusion

The history and background of the Divine Mercy devotion are deeply intertwined with the extraordinary life of St. Faustina Kowalska, whose mystical experiences and messages from Jesus Christ have left an indelible mark on the Catholic faith. The Divine Mercy devotion stands as a testament to the boundless love and mercy of God, offering a message of hope, forgiveness, and compassion that continues to touch the hearts of countless believers worldwide. St. Faustina's legacy lives on, inspiring others to trust in the mercy of God and share that message with the world, one prayer at a time.

theological basis for the Chaplet

The Divine Mercy Chaplet holds a profound theological basis that is not only rooted in the rich traditions of the Catholic faith but is also of utmost importance in modern Catholic spirituality. This compelling theological foundation and its contemporary relevance are as follows:

Biblical Roots: At the core of the Divine Mercy devotion lies the message of God's mercy and love, which has deep roots in the Bible. The very essence of this devotion can be traced back to numerous passages in the Holy Scriptures, particularly emphasizing the themes of forgiveness, compassion, and God's infinite love. It is in the Bible that we find the parables of the Prodigal Son, the Good Shepherd, and the Lost Coin, all of which echo the themes of God's mercy and the return of the sinner.

Theological Virtues of Faith and Trust: The Divine Mercy Chaplet underscores the theological virtues of faith and trust. By repeating the phrase, "Jesus, I trust in You," the Chaplet not only expresses faith in God's mercy but also encourages believers to place their trust in Him. In an age marked by anxiety and doubt, these virtues hold particular significance. The Chaplet teaches that faith and trust are not merely abstract concepts but practical and transformative attitudes in the life of a believer.

Salvation and Redemption: The Chaplet serves as a powerful reminder of the core Christian belief in the salvation and redemption offered through Christ's sacrifice on the Cross. It acknowledges human sinfulness while emphasizing the possibility of reconciliation and redemption through God's mercy. In a world that often grapples with guilt, shame, and the search for meaning, the Divine Mercy devotion provides a profound path to healing and restoration.

Sacramental Focus: Catholic spirituality is deeply sacramental, and the Divine Mercy devotion reinforces this aspect. The Chaplet encourages the use of sacramentals such as the image of the Divine Mercy and the Rosary, reminding believers of the importance of physical reminders and rituals in their spiritual journey. This connection to the sacramental life of the Church offers a tangible means of encountering the divine in the midst of the material world.

Compassion and Outreach: The Divine Mercy devotion extends beyond personal spirituality; it emphasizes the importance of showing mercy and compassion to others. In a contemporary world marked by division and strife, the message of reaching out to others with God's mercy is more relevant than ever. The Chaplet inspires believers to become instruments of God's love and compassion in their interactions with the world.

Universal Prayer for Humanity: The Divine Mercy Chaplet is a universal prayer for the salvation of all souls, emphasizing the catholicity of the Catholic Church. It's a prayer that can be offered for the entire world, transcending boundaries of language, culture, and nationality. In a globalized and interconnected world, the Chaplet reminds us of our shared humanity and the need for a common prayer for mercy and peace.

Intercession of Saints: St. Faustina's canonization and the recognition of the Divine Mercy devotion by the Catholic Church highlight the significance of intercessory prayer and the communion of saints in modern Catholic spirituality. The Chaplet invokes the intercession of St. Faustina and encourages believers to seek the intercession of the saints in their spiritual journey.

In conclusion, the Divine Mercy Chaplet is firmly grounded in the theological foundations of the Catholic faith. Its emphasis on God's mercy, the virtues of faith and trust, the sacramental life of the Church, compassion for others, and universal intercession all make it a powerful and relevant spiritual practice in the modern world. In a time when people seek meaning, healing, and connection, the Divine Mercy devotion offers a path that leads them to the heart of God's inexhaustible mercy, embodying the very essence of what it means to be Catholic in the 21st century.

3

The Chaplet's Structure and Components

The Divine Mercy Chaplet is a beautiful and deeply meaningful prayer in the Catholic tradition, consisting of specific prayers and meditations. Let's provide a detailed breakdown of the Chaplet's prayers, including the introductory and concluding prayers:

Introductory Prayer:

"In the Name of the Father, and of the Son, and of the Holy Spirit. Amen."

The Chaplet begins with the sign of the Cross, invoking the Holy Trinity. It reminds the believer of their faith in the Triune God — Father, Son, and Holy Spirit.

Prayer on the Crucifix:

"Our Father, who art in heaven, hallowed be Thy name; Thy

kingdom come; Thy will be done on earth as it is in heaven. Give us this day our daily bread; and forgive us our trespasses as we forgive those who trespass against us; and lead us not into temptation, but deliver us from evil. Amen."

This is the well-known Our Father, or the Lord's Prayer. It is a central prayer in Christianity, given by Jesus himself, and it sets the tone for the Chaplet. By asking for God's will to be done and seeking forgiveness, it aligns the believer with the themes of mercy and reconciliation.

Prayer on the Large Bead (First Decade):

"Eternal Father, I offer You the Body and Blood, Soul and Divinity of Your dearly beloved Son, Our Lord Jesus Christ, in atonement for our sins and those of the whole world."

In this prayer, the believer offers the Father the very essence of Christ's sacrifice, seeking atonement for their sins and the sins of the world. It focuses on the redemptive aspect of Christ's suffering and the power of His sacrifice for the forgiveness of sins.

On the Ten Small Beads (Decades):

"For the sake of His sorrowful Passion, have mercy on us and on the whole world."

This prayer is recited on each of the ten small beads of the Chaplet. It emphasizes the importance of Christ's suffering (His Passion) and pleads for God's mercy, not only for the person praying but for the entire world. It is a cry for universal mercy and redemption.

Concluding Prayer (after five decades):

"Holy God, Holy Mighty One, Holy Immortal One, have mercy on us and on the whole world."

This prayer acknowledges the holiness and immortality of God and concludes the Chaplet with a final plea for His mercy upon all. It is a powerful declaration of faith in the holiness and mercy of God.

Closing Sign of the Cross:

"In the Name of the Father, and of the Son, and of the Holy Spirit. Amen."

The Chaplet ends as it began, with the sign of the Cross, emphasizing the belief in the Holy Trinity.

The Divine Mercy Chaplet's structure is deliberate and deeply theological. It begins by invoking the Trinity, aligning the believer with the Lord's Prayer, emphasizing God's will, forgiveness, and then proceeds to meditate on the redemptive power of Christ's Passion. It repeatedly pleads for God's mercy on the individual and the entire world, underlining the universality of God's love and forgiveness.

The Chaplet is not just a rote recitation of prayers but a spiritual journey that echoes the core Christian message of salvation, redemption, and the boundless mercy of God. Through its prayers, believers are invited to enter into the mystery of God's mercy, reflect on the sacrifice of Christ, and actively participate in the intercession for the world's need for God's mercy and forgiveness. It's a devotion that encapsulates the essence of Christianity: faith, forgiveness, and the transformative power of God's love.

significance of the Divine Mercy image and the importance of intention in prayer

The Divine Mercy image holds profound significance in the Catholic faith, serving as a visual representation of God's boundless love and mercy. Its importance goes beyond mere aesthetics; it conveys deep theological and spiritual messages. Additionally, the intention in prayer is a fundamental aspect of the Divine Mercy devotion, as it guides the believer's mindset and plays a critical role in the efficacy of the prayer.

The Significance of the Divine Mercy Image:

Visual Representation of God's Mercy: The Divine Mercy image depicts Jesus Christ with His right hand raised in blessing and His left hand touching His heart, from which emanate two rays: one red and one pale. The red ray symbolizes the Blood of Jesus, and the pale ray represents the Water of Baptism. This imagery visually conveys the theological concept that Christ's sacrifice on the Cross, symbolized by His Sacred Heart, provides redemption and purification through His Blood and the waters of Baptism.

Theological Emphasis on Trust: Beneath the image are the words "Jesus, I trust in You." This phrase encapsulates one of the central messages of the Divine Mercy devotion: trust in God's mercy. The image visually reinforces this message, reminding believers to place their trust in the Divine Mercy, even in the face of doubt or despair.

Call to Repentance and Conversion: The image serves as a reminder of the call to repentance and conversion. The outstretched hand of Jesus, offering His blessing, beckons individuals to turn towards Him, seek His forgiveness, and experience spiritual transformation. The Divine Mercy image invites the viewer to approach God with a contrite heart.

Visual Aid for Meditation: The image provides a focal point for meditation and contemplation during the Chaplet or other prayers. By fixing one's gaze on the Divine Mercy image, believers are encouraged to enter into a state of spiritual reflection and deepen their connection with God's mercy.

The Importance of Intention in Prayer:

Mindful Connection with God: Intention in prayer is the conscious focus and purpose with which one approaches God. It is a vital aspect of any prayer, including the Divine Mercy Chaplet. Intention ensures that the prayer is not a mechanical recitation of words but a meaningful conversation with the Divine.

Alignment with Personal Needs: Through intention, individuals bring their specific needs, concerns, and desires before God. In the Divine Mercy Chaplet, one can offer intentions for the healing of a loved one, forgiveness, peace in the world, or any personal need. This makes the prayer deeply personal and relevant to the individual.

Deepening Faith and Trust: Intention in prayer reflects one's trust in God's mercy. By articulating one's intentions, the believer expresses confidence that God listens and responds to their needs. This act of entrusting one's concerns to God strengthens faith and trust in His loving care.

Empathy and Compassion: Intention in prayer is not limited to personal needs but extends to intercessory prayer for others. The Divine Mercy Chaplet allows believers to offer prayers for the needs of the whole world, reflecting an attitude of empathy and compassion toward the suffering of others.

Unity in Communal Prayer: When prayed in a group or community, intention in prayer unites individuals in a common purpose. It fosters a sense of solidarity and shared supplication, as believers come together to seek God's mercy for similar intentions.

In summary, the Divine Mercy image serves as a powerful visual representation of God's mercy, emphasizing trust, repentance, and the call to conversion. Intention in prayer, on the other hand, infuses depth and personal relevance into the Divine Mercy Chaplet. It allows believers to bring their specific needs and intercessions before God, deepening their connection with the Divine and fostering a sense of unity and compassion within the faith community. These two elements work in harmony to make the Divine Mercy devotion a deeply meaningful and transformative aspect of Catholic spirituality.

4

How to Begin Praying the Chaplet

Preparing for and initiating the Divine Mercy Chaplet is a beautiful way to engage in a profound prayer of mercy and grace. Here's a step-by-step guide on how to prepare for and initiate the Chaplet:

Step 1: Find a Quiet and Sacred Space

Choose a quiet and peaceful place where you can pray without distractions. This space can be a corner in your home, a garden, or a nearby church. Ensure that it's a place where you can focus your heart and mind on prayer.

Step 2: Obtain the Necessary Materials

You'll need a few essential materials:

A Divine Mercy image or a representation of Jesus with His heart and the rays (optional but highly recommended for focus and meditation).

A standard Rosary or Divine Mercy beads. If using standard Rosary beads, you can adapt them for the Chaplet by knowing which beads correspond to which prayers.

Step 3: Set the Intention for Your Prayer

Before starting the Chaplet, set a specific intention or intentions for your prayer. You can pray for personal needs, the needs of your loved ones, healing, forgiveness, peace, or any other intention close to your heart. Your intention gives your prayer a purpose and adds a personal touch to it.

Step 4: Begin with the Sign of the Cross

Make the Sign of the Cross while saying: "In the Name of the Father, and of the Son, and of the Holy Spirit. Amen." This is a common Catholic practice and signifies the invocation of the Holy Trinity.

Step 5: Pray the Opening Prayer

Recite the introductory prayer on the crucifix: "Our Father, who art in heaven, hallowed be Thy name; Thy kingdom come; Thy will be done on earth as it is in heaven. Give us this day our daily bread; and forgive us our trespasses as we forgive those who trespass against us; and lead us not into temptation, but deliver us from evil. Amen."

Step 6: Pray the First Decade

On the first bead, pray: "Eternal Father, I offer You the Body and Blood, Soul and Divinity of Your dearly beloved Son, Our Lord

Jesus Christ, in atonement for our sins and those of the whole world."

On the ten small beads, pray: "For the sake of His sorrowful Passion, have mercy on us and on the whole world."

Repeat this process for the remaining four decades (five in total). The prayers on the small beads are often said on standard Rosary beads.

Step 7: Conclude with the Final Prayer

After completing all five decades, pray the concluding prayer: "Holy God, Holy Mighty One, Holy Immortal One, have mercy on us and on the whole world."

Step 8: Repeat the Concluding Sign of the Cross

Close the Chaplet with the Sign of the Cross: "In the Name of the Father, and of the Son, and of the Holy Spirit. Amen."

Step 9: Reflect on Your Intentions

After completing the Divine Mercy Chaplet, take a moment to reflect on the intentions you set at the beginning. Consider the meaning of the prayers you recited and the message of God's mercy. Spend some time in silent reflection or meditation.

Step 10: Make it a Regular Practice

The Divine Mercy Chaplet is a beautiful prayer that can be incorporated into your daily or weekly routine. The more you practice it, the deeper your connection with God's mercy will become.

Remember that the Divine Mercy Chaplet is a powerful prayer that invites you to seek God's mercy, offer your intentions, and reflect on His boundless love. It's a beautiful way to draw closer to God and experience His grace in your life.

5

Praying the Chaplet: A Closer Look

The Divine Mercy Chaplet consists of five decades, each associated with a specific set of prayers and intentions. These decades help believers meditate on different aspects of Christ's Passion and Mercy. Let's explore each decade in-depth, including the prayers and intentions:

First Decade: The Agony of Christ in the Garden of Gethsemane

Prayer for the Decade:

"Eternal Father, I offer You the Body and Blood, Soul and Divinity of Your dearly beloved Son, Our Lord Jesus Christ, in atonement for our sins and those of the whole world."
Intention:

The intention for this decade is to meditate on and seek God's mercy for the agonizing moments in the Garden of Gethsemane. It is a reflection on Christ's sorrow and struggle, as He prayed to the Father for the cup of suffering to pass from Him. Believers can pray for their own moments of anguish and for those who are suffering or struggling with difficult decisions. It is an appeal to God's mercy for strength in times of personal struggle and for all who face similar challenges.

Second Decade: The Scourging at the Pillar

Prayer for the Decade:

"For the sake of His sorrowful Passion, have mercy on us and on the whole world."

Intention:

In this decade, the focus is on the scourging of Jesus at the pillar. Believers reflect on the physical suffering and humiliation Jesus endured. The intention is to seek God's mercy for the healing of physical and emotional wounds, both for oneself and for others. It is also a plea for mercy for those who inflict pain and suffering upon others. This decade emphasizes the idea that through Christ's suffering, healing and redemption are made possible.

Third Decade: The Crowning with Thorns

Prayer for the Decade:

"For the sake of His sorrowful Passion, have mercy on us and on the whole world."

Intention:

This decade centers on the crowning of Jesus with thorns, a symbol of the mockery and cruelty He endured. Believers meditate on the indignities Jesus suffered at the hands of the Roman soldiers. The intention is to seek God's mercy for the healing of emotional and psychological wounds, including those caused by ridicule, humiliation, or mental anguish. It is also a plea for mercy for those who suffer from mental health challenges and for a world where compassion and understanding can replace cruelty and scorn.

Fourth Decade: The Carrying of the Cross

Prayer for the Decade:

"For the sake of His sorrowful Passion, have mercy on us and on the whole world."

Intention:

In this decade, believers reflect on the painful journey of Jesus as He carried the Cross to His crucifixion. The intention is to seek God's mercy for strength during life's burdens and challenges, including carrying one's own crosses. It is also a plea for mercy for those who face physical or emotional burdens, such as illness, grief, or suffering. The carrying of the Cross represents a call for divine assistance in carrying the burdens of life and a reminder of Christ's presence during our struggles.

Fifth Decade: The Crucifixion and Death of Jesus

Prayer for the Decade:

"For the sake of His sorrowful Passion, have mercy on us and on the whole world."

Intention:

This final decade reflects on the crucifixion and death of Jesus. It is a contemplation of the ultimate sacrifice and the source of

God's infinite mercy. The intention is to seek God's mercy for the forgiveness of sins and the salvation of souls. It is a plea for God's mercy to encompass all of humanity, embracing all who are in need of His love and grace. This decade emphasizes the central message of the Divine Mercy devotion: that through Christ's Passion and death, God's mercy is extended to all.

In conclusion, the Divine Mercy Chaplet's five decades guide believers through a contemplative journey of Christ's Passion and Mercy. Each decade encourages deep reflection on different aspects of Jesus' suffering and invites believers to offer specific intentions for personal healing, strength, and forgiveness, as well as for the well-being and salvation of the entire world. It is a profoundly meaningful and transformative prayer that encourages believers to trust in God's boundless mercy.

6

Special Intentions and Novena

The Divine Mercy Novena is a powerful and deeply spiritual Catholic tradition that spans nine days of prayer. It is based on the messages of Jesus to St. Faustina Kowalska, a Polish nun who received divine revelations about God's infinite mercy. Here's a compelling explanation of the Divine Mercy Novena and how to pray it over nine days:

Explanation of the Divine Mercy Novena:

The Divine Mercy Novena is a devotion that prepares the faithful for the celebration of Divine Mercy Sunday, which falls on the Sunday following Easter Sunday. This novena is inspired by the writings and diary of St. Faustina, who received messages and visions of Jesus emphasizing His boundless love and mercy for humanity. The novena consists of nine days of prayer and reflection, focusing on different aspects of God's mercy.

How to Pray the Divine Mercy Novena over Nine Days:

Day 1 - Good Friday: The First Day of the Novena

On the first day, pray the Divine Mercy Chaplet (you can find guidance on how to pray it in previous responses).
Offer your prayer for all mankind and especially for sinners.

Day 2: The Second Day of the Novena

Pray the Divine Mercy Chaplet.
Offer your prayer for priests and religious, that they may be a vessel of God's mercy.

Day 3: The Third Day of the Novena

Pray the Divine Mercy Chaplet.
Offer your prayer for all devout and faithful souls, particularly those who have a deep reverence for God's mercy.

Day 4: The Fourth Day of the Novena

Pray the Divine Mercy Chaplet.
Offer your prayer for those who do not believe in God and those who do not yet know Jesus.

Day 5: The Fifth Day of the Novena

Pray the Divine Mercy Chaplet.
Offer your prayer for those who have separated themselves from the Church, that they may find their way back to God's mercy and love.

Day 6: The Sixth Day of the Novena

Pray the Divine Mercy Chaplet.
Offer your prayer for meek and humble souls and the souls of little children.

Day 7: The Seventh Day of the Novena

Pray the Divine Mercy Chaplet.
Offer your prayer for those who venerate and glorify Jesus' mercy.

Day 8: The Eighth Day of the Novena

Pray the Divine Mercy Chaplet.
Offer your prayer for the souls who are detained in purgatory, that they may soon be united with God's eternal love.

Day 9 - Divine Mercy Sunday: The Final Day of the Novena

Pray the Divine Mercy Chaplet.
On this day, offer your prayer for all people, living and deceased, especially those who are most in need of God's mercy.

Concluding Prayer:

Conclude the novena with a heartfelt thanksgiving to Jesus for His infinite mercy and love. Ask for His blessings and grace upon your life and the lives of those you've prayed for during the nine days.

Attending Mass and Receiving the Eucharist:

On Divine Mercy Sunday, attend Mass if possible and receive the Holy Eucharist, as it is a significant part of the devotion. This day is known as a day of extraordinary graces, and those who receive the Eucharist and fulfill the conditions set by the Church may receive the promise of complete forgiveness of sins and temporal punishment (plenary indulgence).

The Divine Mercy Novena is a beautiful and spiritually enriching tradition that leads believers on a journey of reflection and prayer, deepening their understanding of God's immense love and mercy. By participating in this novena, one can draw closer to the Divine Mercy and experience its transformative power in their life.

Day 1 – Good Friday: The First Day of the Novena
Intention: For all mankind, especially for sinners

Chaplet Prayer:

Begin with the Sign of the Cross: "In the Name of the Father, and of the Son, and of the Holy Spirit. Amen."
Our Father, Hail Mary, and the Apostles' Creed
Pray the Divine Mercy Chaplet:

"Eternal Father, I offer You the Body and Blood, Soul and Divinity of Your dearly beloved Son, Our Lord Jesus Christ, in atonement for our sins and those of the whole world."

On each of the 10 small beads, say: "For the sake of His sorrowful Passion, have mercy on us and on the whole world."
Concluding Prayer:

"Holy God, Holy Mighty One, Holy Immortal One, have mercy on us and on the whole world."

Conclude with the Sign of the Cross: "In the Name of the Father, and of the Son, and of the Holy Spirit. Amen."
Day 2: The Second Day of the Novena
Intention: For priests and religious

Day 3: The Third Day of the Novena
Intention: For all devout and faithful souls

Day 4: The Fourth Day of the Novena
Intention: For those who do not believe in God and those who do not yet know Jesus

Day 5: The Fifth Day of the Novena
Intention: For those who have separated themselves from the Church

Day 6: The Sixth Day of the Novena
Intention: For meek and humble souls, and the souls of little children

Day 7: The Seventh Day of the Novena
Intention: For those who venerate and glorify Jesus' mercy

Day 8: The Eighth Day of the Novena
Intention: For the souls who are detained in purgatory

Day 9 – Divine Mercy Sunday: The Final Day of the Novena
Intention: For all people, living and deceased, especially those who are most in need of God's mercy

Chaplet Prayer for Day 9:

Begin with the Sign of the Cross: "In the Name of the Father, and of the Son, and of the Holy Spirit. Amen."
Our Father, Hail Mary, and the Apostles' Creed
Pray the Divine Mercy Chaplet:

"Eternal Father, I offer You the Body and Blood, Soul and Divinity of Your dearly beloved Son, Our Lord Jesus Christ, in atonement for our sins and those of the whole world."

On each of the 10 small beads, say: "For the sake of His sorrowful Passion, have mercy on us and on the whole world."

Concluding Prayer:

"Holy God, Holy Mighty One, Holy Immortal One, have mercy on us and on the whole world."

Conclude with the Sign of the Cross: "In the Name of the Father, and of the Son, and of the Holy Spirit. Amen."

On Divine Mercy Sunday, attend Mass, receive the Holy Eucharist, and fulfill the conditions set by the Church for receiving the plenary indulgence and complete forgiveness of sins.

7

The Promises and Graces of the Chaplet

The Divine Mercy Chaplet is a profound and spiritually enriching devotion within the Catholic faith, closely associated with promises and blessings. These promises and blessings are inspired by the revelations of Jesus to St. Faustina Kowalska and are meant to encourage the faithful to embrace the infinite love and mercy of God. Here is a compelling discussion of the promises and blessings associated with the Divine Mercy Chaplet:

1. Complete Forgiveness of Sins:

One of the most prominent promises associated with the Divine Mercy Chaplet is the assurance of complete forgiveness of sins. Jesus, in His messages to St. Faustina, made it clear that those who pray the Chaplet with a contrite heart will receive the grace of complete pardon for their sins. This promise underscores the transformative power of God's mercy, offering a fresh start to those who seek His forgiveness.

2. Relief from Suffering and Grief:

Another promise of the Divine Mercy Chaplet is the alleviation of suffering and grief. It's a source of solace and comfort for those who are going through difficult times, whether it's physical, emotional, or spiritual suffering. By praying the Chaplet, individuals can find consolation in the compassionate heart of Jesus.

3. Protection from God's Wrath:

The Divine Mercy Chaplet emphasizes God's desire to shield souls from His divine wrath. Jesus implores humanity to turn to His mercy and not be afraid of His justice. This promise reassures believers that they can rely on God's mercy as a shelter from judgment and punishment.

4. Grace at the Hour of Death:

Praying the Divine Mercy Chaplet regularly offers the grace of being well-prepared for the moment of death. It promises a peaceful and grace-filled transition into the afterlife. This is especially comforting for those who want to ensure that their souls are in a state of grace when facing the unknown.

5. Conversion of Sinners:

Through the Divine Mercy Chaplet, believers are called to intercede for the conversion of sinners. This prayer has the potential to touch the hearts of those who have strayed from the path of faith and lead them back to God's mercy. It underscores the Chaplet's role in spreading God's compassion and forgiveness to all.

6. An Outpouring of God's Grace:

The Divine Mercy Chaplet is also associated with the promise of an outpouring of God's grace upon those who pray it with a sincere heart. This grace encompasses both spiritual and temporal blessings, which can profoundly impact one's life, bringing forth divine favor and providence.

7. An Opportunity for Spiritual Growth:

Through the consistent practice of the Divine Mercy Chaplet, individuals can experience spiritual growth and a deepening of their relationship with God. It serves as a conduit for personal transformation and increased holiness.

Real-life stories and testimonials of individuals who have experienced the transformative power of the Divine Mercy Chaplet are a testament to the profound impact this prayer can have on people's lives. Here are a few compelling stories:

1. Healing from Addiction:

John, a recovering alcoholic, struggled for years with addiction. He felt hopeless and believed he was beyond redemption. One day, a friend introduced him to the Divine Mercy Chaplet. John began praying it daily, asking for the strength to overcome his addiction. Over time, he found the support he needed, attended Alcoholics Anonymous meetings, and credited the Chaplet for his newfound strength. Today, John is sober and helping others in their recovery journey.

2. Reconciliation in a Broken Family:

Sarah's family was torn apart by a bitter feud that had lasted for years. After her mother's death, Sarah decided to pray the Divine Mercy Chaplet, asking for reconciliation and forgiveness within her family. Slowly, her siblings began to soften their hearts, and eventually, they reconciled. The Chaplet played a significant role in healing deep-seated wounds, and the family's bond was restored.

3. A Miraculous Recovery:

Mary, a woman diagnosed with a severe and life-threatening illness, had exhausted all medical treatments. She turned to her faith and began praying the Divine Mercy Chaplet daily. To the astonishment of her doctors, Mary's condition improved significantly, and she eventually went into remission. Her doctors couldn't explain it, but Mary believed that it was the divine intervention she had prayed for.

4. Finding Purpose through Acts of Mercy:

Tom, a retired man who had been feeling lost and purposeless, began to pray the Divine Mercy Chaplet regularly. As he meditated on God's mercy, he felt called to perform acts of mercy in his community. He started volunteering at a local soup kitchen and visiting the elderly in nursing homes. Through these acts of mercy, he found a new sense of purpose and fulfillment in his retirement years.

5. Peace in the Midst of Grief:

After the sudden loss of her son in a tragic accident, Maria was consumed by grief and despair. A friend shared the Divine Mercy Chaplet with her. Through the prayer and meditation on God's mercy, Maria found a source of solace and strength. While the pain of her loss remained, she discovered a profound inner peace that helped her cope with her grief.

6. Conversion and Renewed Faith:

Michael, an agnostic, was searching for meaning in his life. He came across the Divine Mercy Chaplet and began to recite it out of curiosity. As he meditated on the prayers and the concept of God's mercy, he experienced a profound conversion. Michael became a devout Catholic and dedicated his life to spreading the message of God's mercy to others.

These real-life stories and testimonials highlight the transformative power of the Divine Mercy Chaplet. They demonstrate how this prayer has the capacity to bring healing, reconciliation, hope, and a renewed sense of faith to individuals facing various challenges and seeking God's mercy in their lives.

8. A Call to Acts of Mercy:

While not a formal promise, the Divine Mercy Chaplet is an invitation to practice acts of mercy in one's own life. By praying for God's mercy on others, individuals are encouraged to embody mercy in their actions and interactions with others, fulfilling Christ's call to "be merciful, just as your Father is merciful."

In conclusion, the Divine Mercy Chaplet is a prayer of profound significance within the Catholic faith. It offers promises and blessings that highlight the all-encompassing nature of God's mercy, His desire for reconciliation, and the transformation of hearts. Through this devotion, believers can find hope, forgiveness, and the assurance of God's eternal love, ultimately deepening their faith and spiritual journey.

8

Praying the Chaplet as a Community

The significance of communal prayer in the context of the Divine Mercy devotion is a testament to the transformative power of collective spirituality and the communal expression of faith. Here are compelling reasons why communal prayer plays a vital role in the Divine Mercy devotion:

Unity and Solidarity: Communal prayer brings individuals together in unity and solidarity. The Divine Mercy devotion emphasizes God's boundless love and mercy for all. When believers come together in communal prayer, they embody this universal message, transcending differences and uniting in their shared faith.

Amplifying Prayer Intentions: In a communal setting, the intentions of each participant are collectively amplified. When a group prays for healing, forgiveness, or grace, the combined intentions create a powerful spiritual energy that resonates with the Divine Mercy message of compassion and love.

Comfort and Support: Communal prayer provides a sense of comfort and support, especially in times of personal suffering or grief. The Divine Mercy devotion, with its emphasis on God's consolation and solace, is particularly meaningful in times of communal prayer. It reminds participants that they are not alone in their trials.

Strengthening Faith: Being part of a community that shares the same faith and devotion can strengthen one's own belief. The Divine Mercy devotion's central theme of trusting in God's mercy is reinforced when individuals witness others expressing the same trust and devotion.

Learning and Sharing: Communal prayer allows participants to learn from one another and share their insights and experiences. This exchange of spiritual wisdom can deepen the understanding of the Divine Mercy message and help individuals grow in their faith.

Intercessory Prayer: The communal aspect of the Divine Mercy devotion encourages intercessory prayer. Participants pray not only for themselves but also for others, seeking God's mercy on behalf of those in need. This selfless act aligns with the message of mercy and compassion.

Building a Spiritual Community: Communal prayer fosters a sense of belonging to a spiritual community. This community supports individuals in their faith journey and can serve as a source of encouragement and accountability.

Witnessing Miracles and Transformations: In communal prayer, participants may witness the transformative power of the Divine Mercy message in the lives of others. Stories of healing, conversion, and miracles can inspire and strengthen the faith of the entire community.

Participation in Liturgical Celebrations: Communal prayer often takes place within the context of liturgical celebrations, such as Divine Mercy Sunday. These events offer the opportunity to receive the sacraments, including the Holy Eucharist, which are integral to the Catholic faith and the Divine Mercy devotion.

Continuation of Tradition: Communal prayer in the context of the Divine Mercy devotion continues a rich tradition within the Catholic Church. It connects contemporary believers with the historical roots of the devotion and strengthens its legacy.

In conclusion, communal prayer is of profound significance in the context of the Divine Mercy devotion. It embodies the core message of God's infinite love and mercy, fostering unity, support, and shared faith among participants. Through communal prayer, believers can experience the transformative power of the Divine Mercy message and collectively bear witness to the boundless compassion of God.

9

Troubleshooting and Common Questions

here are answers to frequently asked questions about the Divine Mercy Chaplet:

1. What is the Divine Mercy Chaplet?

The Divine Mercy Chaplet is a Christian prayer, primarily within the Catholic tradition, that focuses on God's infinite mercy and compassion. It consists of specific prayers and meditations designed to invoke God's mercy for oneself and the whole world.

2. How do I pray the Divine Mercy Chaplet?

To pray the Divine Mercy Chaplet, you'll need a set of rosary beads or a Divine Mercy Chaplet rosary. Begin with the Sign of the Cross, followed by the recitation of the Our Father, Hail Mary, and Apostles' Creed. Then, on the large beads, pray the introductory prayer, followed by the Divine Mercy Chaplet prayers on the small beads.

3. What are the Divine Mercy Chaplet prayers?

The Divine Mercy Chaplet prayers consist of an introductory prayer, followed by the repetition of the phrase "For the sake of His sorrowful Passion, have mercy on us and on the whole world" on each of the ten small beads. The Chaplet concludes with the concluding prayer, "Holy God, Holy Mighty One, Holy Immortal One, have mercy on us and on the whole world."

4. When is the Divine Mercy Chaplet typically prayed?

The Divine Mercy Chaplet can be prayed at any time, but it holds special significance on Divine Mercy Sunday, which falls on the Sunday following Easter Sunday. It's also prayed during the Divine Mercy Novena, which begins on Good Friday and leads up to Divine Mercy Sunday.

5. What is the significance of the Divine Mercy image in the Chaplet?

The Divine Mercy image, with the phrase "Jesus, I trust in You," is often associated with the Chaplet. It's a visual representation of God's mercy, showing Jesus with rays of red and white light emanating from His heart. The image serves as a focal point for meditation and a reminder of God's boundless love and compassion.

6. Can I pray the Divine Mercy Chaplet for specific intentions?

Yes, you can incorporate personal intentions into the Divine Mercy Chaplet. Each day of the Divine Mercy Novena, you can assign specific intentions for your prayers, focusing on various aspects of God's mercy and seeking His grace for particular needs.

7. What are the promises associated with the Divine Mercy Chaplet?

The Divine Mercy Chaplet is associated with several promises, including complete forgiveness of sins, relief from suffering, protection from God's wrath, grace at the hour of death, and conversion of sinners. These promises emphasize the transformative power of God's mercy and love.

Tips for overcoming common challenges and distractions during prayer

Overcoming common challenges and distractions during prayer is a universal struggle, but with practice and patience, you can develop techniques to maintain focus and deepen your spiritual connection. Here are compelling tips to help you overcome these challenges:

1. Set the Right Environment:

Choose a quiet, comfortable, and well-lit space for prayer.
   Remove distractions, such as phones or noisy objects.
   2. Create a Routine:

Establish a consistent time for prayer each day.
   Routine helps your mind and body prepare for prayer.
   3. Start with Relaxation:

Begin with deep, calming breaths.
   Relax your body and clear your mind of stress.
   4. Use Prayer Aids:

Utilize prayer books, images, or candles to focus your attention.

Physical aids can help anchor your thoughts.
5. Structure Your Prayers:

Choose specific prayers or a prayer format.
   This gives your mind a clear path to follow.
   6. Be Mindful of Your Posture:

Maintain a comfortable and upright posture.
   Good posture can help you stay alert and focused.
   7. Address Distractions Gently:

If your mind wanders, gently bring it back to your prayer.
   Don't be too critical of yourself.
   8. Use Visualization:

Picture scenes from scripture or your prayers.
   Visualization can make your prayers more vivid.
   9. Engage the Senses:

Light incense, play soft music, or use religious art.
   Engaging the senses can create a sacred atmosphere.
   10. Recite Aloud:
   - Pray your words aloud.
   - The act of speaking can enhance concentration.

11. Keep a Prayer Journal:
   - Write down your thoughts and reflections.
   - Journaling helps you process your experiences.

12. Break Longer Prayers:
   - If you're distracted during a long prayer, break it into shorter

segments.
   - Focus on one segment at a time.

13. Seek Guidance:
    - Consult a spiritual director or mentor.
    - They can provide insights to enhance your prayer life.

14. Understand Common Distractions:
    - Recognize common distractions like worries, to-do lists, or past events.
    - Acknowledging them helps you let go.

15. Practice Mindfulness:
    - Learn mindfulness techniques.
    - Mindfulness can help you stay present in the moment.

16. Repeat a Mantra:
    - Choose a single word or phrase to repeat.
    - This can help maintain your concentration.

17. Offer the Distractions:
    - When you're distracted, offer those thoughts and concerns to God.
    - Use them as a way to connect with the Divine.

18. Join a Prayer Group:
    - Praying with a group can provide mutual support.
    - Group prayer can help you stay focused.

19. Prioritize Prayer:
    - Treat prayer as a priority, not an afterthought.

- Understand its importance in your spiritual journey.

20. Practice Patience:
    - Overcoming distractions takes time and practice.
    - Be patient with yourself and your progress.

Remember that the journey to deepening your prayer life and overcoming distractions is a gradual process. Be kind to yourself and know that every moment of sincere prayer, even when faced with distractions, is a step closer to a deeper connection with the Divine.

8. Is the Divine Mercy Chaplet only for Catholics?

While the Divine Mercy Chaplet has deep roots in the Catholic tradition, individuals of various Christian denominations and even non-Catholics are encouraged to pray it. The central message of God's mercy is universal and inclusive, meant for all who seek His love and forgiveness.

9. What is the difference between the Divine Mercy Chaplet and the Rosary?

The Divine Mercy Chaplet and the Rosary are both prayer traditions in the Catholic faith, but they have distinct prayers and meditations. The Rosary is dedicated to the life of Jesus and the Virgin Mary, while the Divine Mercy Chaplet focuses on God's mercy and the redemption of humanity.

10. How can I deepen my connection with the Divine Mercy through the Chaplet?

To deepen your connection with the Divine Mercy through the Chaplet, maintain a consistent prayer routine, meditate on the significance of God's mercy, and incorporate acts of mercy into your daily life. Consider joining a faith community to share your spiritual journey with others.

10

Living the Divine Mercy Message

The Divine Mercy Chaplet and the Divine Mercy devotion offer a profound and transformative message of God's boundless love and mercy. Integrating these practices into daily life can lead to a deeper spiritual connection and a life infused with the grace of mercy. Here's a compelling reflection on how the Chaplet and the Divine Mercy devotion can be integrated into daily life:

A Message of Mercy in Daily Living:
   The Divine Mercy devotion is not confined to a particular time or place; it is a way of life. Its message of God's infinite love and mercy is an invitation to live each day with the awareness of this profound truth. As we rise each morning, we can begin by acknowledging God's mercy and expressing our gratitude for the gift of a new day.

The Chaplet as a Daily Anchor:
   Incorporating the Divine Mercy Chaplet into daily life is a tangible way to connect with God's mercy. As we recite the Chaplet, we remind ourselves of the central message that Jesus

gave to St. Faustina: "Jesus, I trust in You." This prayer becomes an anchor, grounding us in faith and trust amid life's uncertainties.

Meditation on Mercy:

The Divine Mercy image, with its rays of red and white light, can serve as a focal point for daily meditation. This image is a visual reminder of God's compassion, inviting us to contemplate the depth of His love and the significance of His mercy. Whether it's a quick glance at the image or a longer meditation, this daily practice can transform our perspective and attitude.

Living Mercy in Our Actions:

The Divine Mercy devotion encourages us to practice acts of mercy in our daily interactions. Small acts of kindness, forgiveness, and compassion are living expressions of God's mercy. By making a conscious effort to be merciful to others, we reflect the Divine Mercy in our own lives.

A Source of Strength and Consolation:

Life is filled with challenges, and moments of suffering and pain are inevitable. The Divine Mercy devotion reminds us that, in those difficult times, we can turn to God's mercy for strength and consolation. Whether it's a health crisis, the loss of a loved one, or personal struggles, the Chaplet can be a source of solace.

The Communal Aspect:

Participating in communal prayer, especially on Divine Mercy Sunday and during the Divine Mercy Novena, connects us with a broader spiritual community. It fosters unity and provides an opportunity to support and be supported by others in our faith journey.

Spreading the Message:
The Divine Mercy message is meant to be shared. By talking to friends and family about the Chaplet and the devotion, we can spread the message of God's mercy to others. Through our words and actions, we become witnesses to the transformative power of God's love and compassion.

Daily Conversion and Renewal:
Incorporating the Divine Mercy devotion into daily life is an ongoing process of conversion and renewal. It challenges us to be better, more compassionate individuals, continually seeking God's mercy and striving to extend that mercy to others.

As we reflect on integrating the Divine Mercy Chaplet and the devotion into daily life, we come to understand that this is more than a routine; it's a way of living. It's a journey of faith that, with each passing day, brings us closer to the profound truth that God's mercy knows no bounds. With each act of mercy, with each prayer, and with each moment of reflection, we become living expressions of this divine message. In our daily lives, we can embody the message, "Jesus, I trust in You," and let God's mercy permeate our hearts, shaping our thoughts, words, and deeds.

Practical advice on embodying the virtues of mercy, forgiveness, and compassion
Embodying the virtues of mercy, forgiveness, and compassion is a noble and transformative journey that can profoundly impact your life and the lives of those around you. Here is some practical

advice on how to cultivate these virtues:

1. Practice Self-Compassion:

Before extending compassion to others, learn to be compassionate toward yourself. Acknowledge your own imperfections and be kind to yourself in times of personal struggle.

2. Cultivate Empathy:

Develop the ability to understand and share the feelings of others. Listen actively when people share their joys and sorrows. Try to put yourself in their shoes.

3. Forgive and Let Go:

Forgiveness is a powerful act of compassion. Forgive not for the sake of others, but for your own peace of mind. Let go of grudges and resentments.

4. Understand Human Weakness:

Recognize that all humans are imperfect and prone to mistakes. Understand that sometimes people hurt others unintentionally, driven by their own fears and insecurities.

5. Be Slow to Judge:

Avoid quick judgments and assumptions about others. Be open to understanding their motives and circumstances before passing judgment.

6. Offer a Listening Ear:

Sometimes, all someone needs is someone to listen without judgment. Offer your presence as a source of comfort and support.

7. Act with Kindness:

Random acts of kindness can go a long way in demonstrating compassion. Hold the door for someone, smile at a stranger, or offer a helping hand.

8. Serve Others:

Volunteer for a cause or charity. Serving others can be a direct way to practice compassion and extend mercy to those in need.

9. Practice Patience:

Patience is a virtue closely tied to compassion. When dealing with others, especially in moments of conflict, strive to remain patient.

10. Educate Yourself:

- Learn about the challenges and struggles faced by different groups of people. Understanding their experiences can deepen your compassion.

11. Reflect on Your Actions:

- Regularly reflect on your interactions and actions. Consider how you could have been more compassionate or forgiving in certain situations.

12. Avoid Gossip and Criticism:

- Refrain from engaging in gossip or speaking negatively about others. Instead, focus on constructive conversations that build others up.

13. Pray for Guidance:

- Seek guidance and strength through prayer or meditation. Many find spiritual practices to be a source of inspiration for embodying virtues like mercy and compassion.

14. Set Boundaries:
 - While compassion is essential, setting boundaries is also important. Recognize when someone's actions or behavior are harmful and take steps to protect yourself.

15. Reflect on Role Models:
 - Identify role models who embody the virtues of mercy, forgiveness, and compassion. Learn from their examples and stories.

16. Seek Reconciliation:
 - When conflicts arise, strive for reconciliation. Forgiving and seeking resolution can mend relationships and promote healing.

17. Learn from Past Mistakes:
 - Embrace the lessons that come from your own mistakes and moments of unkindness. Use them as opportunities for personal growth.

18. Be Mindful:
 - Practice mindfulness to stay present in the moment. It helps you respond to others with greater awareness and compassion.

19. Surround Yourself with Positive Influences:
 - Spend time with people who encourage and exemplify these virtues. Positive influences can reinforce your commitment to embodying mercy, forgiveness, and compassion.

20. Make it a Daily Intention:
 - Set the intention each day to embody these virtues. Be mindful of opportunities to practice them in your interactions with others.

Embodying mercy, forgiveness, and compassion is a lifelong journey, but it's one that enriches your own life and the lives of those you touch. As you consistently practice these virtues, you not only become a source of healing and comfort to others but also experience a deep sense of fulfillment and spiritual growth in your own life.

11

Conclusion

Dear Seeker of God's Mercy,

In the depths of your heart, you have encountered the transformative power of the Divine Mercy Chaplet, a prayer that echoes the very heartbeat of God's love and compassion. As you journey along this path, remember that your quest for divine mercy is a noble and sacred one.

In moments of doubt or distraction, recall the promises that accompany the Chaplet - the complete forgiveness of sins, the relief from suffering, and the grace at the hour of death. These promises are not mere words but living expressions of God's desire to draw you closer to His boundless love.

Know that every bead of the Chaplet is a step closer to God's embrace. Each repetition of 'For the sake of His sorrowful Passion, have mercy on us and on the whole world' is a whispered plea, a testament to your trust in the Divine. In this prayer, you surrender your burdens and seek solace in the ever-open arms of God.

As you continue your journey, understand that growth in faith is not always linear. There will be days when distractions cloud your mind, and doubts may linger. Yet, it is precisely in these moments that your determination and commitment to prayer are most profound.

Consider the Divine Mercy image, where Jesus, with His heart radiating red and white rays, gazes upon you with eyes full of love and understanding. He, who knows your deepest sorrows and joys, never wavers in His commitment to walk beside you on this path of mercy.

Your daily practice of the Divine Mercy Chaplet is not just a routine; it is an unwavering testament of your faith, an expression of your yearning for God's mercy to fill every corner of your life.

Remember that your relationship with God is an evolving journey. Just as a tree grows stronger over time, your connection with the Divine deepens with every prayer, every moment of compassion, and every act of mercy.

So, keep your heart open to the endless reservoir of divine grace. Continue to be a source of compassion and forgiveness in the lives of others, for in doing so, you are a living reflection of the mercy that flows from God's heart to yours.

In moments of darkness, when you feel distant from God's mercy, recall the words of the Chaplet: 'Jesus, I trust in You.' These words are your lifeline, a declaration of unwavering trust in the One who never abandons His children.

With each bead, with each whispered prayer, you reaffirm your place in the loving embrace of God. Continue on this path of mercy, for it leads to a deeper understanding of God's love, a greater capacity for forgiveness, and a life enriched with compassion.

You are not alone on this journey. Countless souls are praying alongside you, and the Divine Mercy devotion unites you with believers around the world. Together, we strengthen each other, becoming beacons of God's mercy.

So, dear seeker, take heart. As you continue to practice the Divine Mercy Chaplet, you are walking in the footsteps of saints and mystics who have known the transformative power of God's mercy. Know that you are cherished and guided, for your pursuit of divine mercy is a testament to the enduring, boundless love of God.

Keep the faith, hold the Chaplet in your hands, and let its prayers flow from your heart. Embrace the mercy that awaits you, and let it mold you into a vessel of divine love. The journey is long, but the destination is eternal, and in God's mercy, you shall find your true home.

With trust and compassion, A Fellow Seeker of God's Mercy"